How To Get Ex Back

The Definitive Guide To Winning Back Your Ex-girlfriend
And Keeping Her For Good

(The Complete Guide To Regaining Your Ex-girlfriend)

Raymundo Johnson

TABLE OF CONTENT

Do You Want Them Back Genuinely? 1

How To Make Your Ex Desire You Once More 5

Acknowledging The Need For A Temporary Withdrawal 19

How To Regain His Confidence 24

Verify That He Is Worth It 28

Understand Why You Desire To Sleep With Him ... 36

Activities For The Thirty-Day Period 49

Allowing One Another Space To Process Things 72

Science Identifies Proven Methods For Overcoming Breakups 88

Take The Initiative 106

The Appointment 119

When Relationships Fail As A Result Of Other Factors 132

Take The Initiative And Accept Responsibility 141

Do You Want Them Back Genuinely?

Let's be honest: the end of a relationship is difficult and problematic. Regardless of the reasons for the breakup, it is never simple for those committed to the relationship. It can flip their universe on its head and turn it inside out. It is so painful because it signifies the end of a relationship, shared aspirations, and shared commitments. A relationship ends when feelings of intense anguish, great disappointment, anger, and grief are present. Recovery can be greatly aided by a list of helpful tips.

You may currently be experiencing sensations of isolation. Maybe you've been thinking that there is no valid reason to live. You feel unworthy without your special someone by your side, and you keep questioning yourself why your relationship failed and what might have been. You are anxious about the upcoming uncertainties.

One of the most crucial steps individuals must take is to embrace the truth and achieve closure. Frequent communication with your ex would not be beneficial. Ensure that you encounter your ex-partner for the final time and express gratitude for the time you've spent together.

Most individuals allow themselves to suffer as a result of the relationship errors they believe they have made. When you feel this way, it's time to stand up and acknowledge that you may have made some errors, but that is never an excuse to feel like a complete failure. Instead, learn from your errors and recognize your strengths. Never permit anyone or any negative experience to drag you down.

If you are still being haunted by the ghosts of your past, seek out ways to avoid them. It may be challenging, but if you believe in yourself, you will undoubtedly succeed. Still, avoid drugs, alcohol, and anything else that could impair your health.

Moreover, associate with trustworthy individuals who hold optimistic worldviews. You can always attempt to express your feelings, but you shouldn't dwell excessively on how you feel about your ex. Instead, try to enjoy conversing about other subjects that matter to you. It would be noble to spend time with family, friends, and support organizations.

Other than that, you can do something you've always desired to do. Cook like a pro, paint like Pablo Picasso, dance like a pro, and acquire additional skills. Consequently, now is the utmost best time to transform negative energies into positive ones and be productive.

Never is it simple to escape the shadows of a past relationship. You can always rely on this list of relationship break-up tips and remember that you have the power to escape your miseries and continue living your life. Healing requires time, and you should not consider a new relationship until you are certain you are ready. Know that there are many more positive experiences forthcoming. Never pass up the possibility to take advantage of such opportunities and improve yourself!

How To Make Your Ex Desire You Once More

You will feel open and exposed immediately after the breakup. Now is not the time to make rash choices. Do nothing that you will quickly come to regret.

Your breakup with your ex will be painful for you. You may not initially believe that you can be joyful, let alone attractive and self-confident. However, if you deliberately act as if you are happy, you WILL shortly feel more joyful and cheerful.

Utilize this time without contact with your ex to concentrate on yourself. You may continue to feel disoriented and desolate. However, you possess the strength and capability to ascend above your current circumstance. Make an effort to constantly remind yourself of this.

If you want your ex to return, you must earn him back. You must make him find you desirable. You must demonstrate that despite the breakup, you are your own person: self-confident, joyful, attractive, and optimistic. He must desire for you to return to his existence.

How do you accomplish this?

Reflect.

This time is best spent addressing your own problems. Take the time to reflect on past events with the goal of formulating a practical plan for self-improvement.

Think positively about this proposal. Do it with a positive attitude. Do not embark on a self-improvement program based on self-criticism. You must recognize that resolving your personal issues will make you happier, more well-adjusted, and more mature.

Find someone with whom you can converse.

Choose a therapist, a member of your family, or a trusted associate. Give your pent-up emotions free reign; rage and weep to release your emotions. Do this with somebody who understands your perspective. This enables you to express your thoughts and emotions without jeopardizing your relationship with your ex-boyfriend irreparably.

Let out your pent-up pains. You will benefit from communicating your emotions. You will experience therapeutic benefits.

By discussing the breakup with a friend, you are able to process your emotions and gain perspective. It will allow you to examine issues from various perspectives. It will help you better comprehend your ex-partner. If you decide to reconcile with your ex, the knowledge you acquire will put you in a stronger position.

Examine your relationship with as much candor, courage, and transparency as possible. Consider both the pros and cons.

Attempt to pinpoint the precise issues predominantly responsible for the relationship's breakdown. Can the issues be resolved? How? If you believe the problems can be resolved, you and your ex can later discuss whether you are both willing and prepared to do what it takes to resolve the issues.

Planned reconciliation may not be worthwhile under certain conditions. Are the circumstances that led to the separation difficult to mend? Are you willing to alter your behavior to foster an improved relationship? If your boyfriend refuses to work on the relationship, it may be prudent to move forward with the breakup.

If you genuinely believe you were the primary cause of the relationship's demise, do not hesitate to apologize when it is time to see your ex again. He will appreciate your gesture. He will experience more affection and benevolence towards you. Admitting your mistakes will assist you in making a positive break with the past.

Enjoy your newfound freedom.

People in relationships typically consider themselves a "couple." They tend to lose some of their independence and individuality. Utilize your time alone to rediscover your independence. Learn to take pleasure in trying new things, exploring new locations, making new friends, and engaging in new, engaging activities. This will result in increased self-confidence and a revitalizing sense of wholeness.

Live a full existence.

Do not place your life on hold while you await the return of your ex. You can do many engaging activities. Learn a skill. Develop a new passion. Register for a class. Join a social or civic group. Make new acquaintances. All of these activities are beneficial to one's self-esteem. You will experience increased productivity, happiness, and confidence.

Reconnect with your old acquaintances.

Typically, girls with boyfriends prioritize their companions over their friendships. The time has come to reconnect with your peers. Date with them. Have joy. Laugh your souls out with abandon. You will quickly realize that life can be enjoyable even without a companion.

Treat yourself well.

Concentrate on your needs and the things that bring you pleasure. Get enough rest. Exercise. Eat healthily. Take lengthy, hot baths. Read excellent books. Take lengthy walks. When you engage in "happy" activities for yourself, you become healthier, more tranquil, and cheerful. You will look and feel great.

Go out on dates.

Even if you are not actively attempting to replace your ex, you should date attractive men. This will increase your self-esteem. When going on outings, you practice your conversational abilities. You reconnect with the charming, flirtatious, and witty aspect of yourself that may have been absent for some time.

Improve yourself.

You have many positive attributes. These may include your physical health, physical appearance, skills, talents, social and emotional abilities. Remind yourself that you possess all of these qualities. This will increase your satisfaction and confidence. Recognize and appreciate your individual worth.

Assess yourself.

You have not communicated with your ex for at least a couple of months. At this point, you should have made progress in several crucial areas.

You've adjusted your priorities.

You are no longer the emotional wreck you were during the separation.

You've taken time to consider yourself and your involvement in the breakup.

You have engaged in a self-improvement and enhancement initiative.

You have decided that, if possible, you want your ex-boyfriend back.

You have recognized that if he does not return to your life, you will still be fine.

You have realized that even without your ex by your side, there are numerous opportunities for love, contentment, and fulfillment.

Do you have a positive opinion of yourself and your existence in general? If you do, you are now prepared to contact your ex.

It is time to determine whether it is possible to reignite the love, care, and attraction that characterized your early relationship.

The next step is to determine whether you share the same feelings for him. Is he still attracted to you in secret? You must reawaken these sentiments and cause him to view you in an exciting new light.

End the no-contact period and contact your ex-partner. Transmit text communications.

According to relationship experts, you should contact your ex by texting, emailing, or penning him a letter. Make an effort to reestablish contact with minimal emotional investment. Try to reignite attraction without inviting rejection or frustration.

In particular, text messages are not menacing. They are brief. The communications can be a lovely combination of the friendly, flirtatious, and personal. You can learn to compose amusing and cunning text messages. You can make your ex enthusiastic about receiving such messages.

Be very discreet with your text message usage. Do not discuss your emotions or how badly you want him back in your life. Do not argue about the breakup or assign responsibility. Always make the communications entertaining and upbeat. Make joyful, positive references to your past by casually mentioning the good times you had together.

Utilize the messages to signify your progression. Inform your ex that you are now content with your existence. You can mention that you are having a good time and meeting new people.

The purpose of text messages is to eliminate his potential perception of you as a failed ex-partner. You wish to replace this image with a more upbeat, entertaining, and appealing one.

Avoid being in a haste. Establish cordial ties at your leisure.

If you can sufficiently pique his interest, he may want to see you again. Otherwise, you may request to see him at the appropriate time.

Visit your ex.

Make certain you do not refer to the event as a date. You do not want to make him feel defensive. You do not want him to realize that you desire his return. You want him to view you as a friend who is willing to apologize for prior transgressions and make amends if necessary.

Utilize the time to build attraction subtly. This should not be challenging. In the past, you were both attracted to one another. It should not be difficult to reignite the attraction, particularly since you have undergone numerous changes that he is likely to find alluring.

Maintain a casual and playful tone. If you were responsible for profoundly hurt emotions, you can offer a sincere apology. Then proceed. Avoid discussing the breakup in depth. Consider your previous relationship with him to be finished.

Stay attractive, sweet, and courteous. Use subtle techniques to make him see you as the beautiful woman he once adored. Utilize a perfume or garment that he cherished. Remind him of the enjoyable occasions you shared together.

If this first "non-date" is enjoyable for both of you, you may wish to continue spending time together. Maintain a strictly welcoming atmosphere. You can dine, view a film, or attend a concert. It is essential to maintain things on an even keel while attempting to reacquaint yourselves and become friends once more.

Remember that this is a new beginning. You are not attempting to restore your previous relationship; rather, you are beginning a brand-new, untainted chapter.

Acknowledging The Need For A Temporary Withdrawal

People who have recently broken up with their partners have a common propensity to bombard their exes with messages that range from simple requests for an apology to desperate pleas for reconciliation. This is completely typical. In fact, this demonstrates the lengths to which individuals would go in an attempt to save their relationships. However, the query is whether this strategy is worthwhile or even effective.

In reality, breakups are never simple. While it is true that some breakups are amicable, the majority of breakups involve a great deal of emotional pain and psychological damage. All of these negative emotions are at their peak between the date of the actual separation and the few days or weeks that follow. This is precisely why a no-contact period is necessary, during which you refrain from communicating with your ex in any way for a predetermined amount of time.

There is no set duration for the period of no contact. Idealistically, however, it should not be shorter than two weeks. Nevertheless, regardless of the duration, you must resist the urge to communicate with your ex without compromise. This is admittedly difficult to accomplish, given that one's presence is no longer merely corporeal. Additionally, the prevalence of email, text messages, and social networks online makes it particularly difficult to neglect your ex. Regardless, you must maintain your resolve and stand steadfast. This is why:

It is not a good idea to attempt to communicate with your ex while the wounds of the past and all associated negative memories are not yet completely resolved. Have you ever attempted to reason with someone who is in an uncontrollable rage? No matter how logical and reasonable you attempt to be, it is impossible to convey your message clearly without being subjected to insults, blame, and other forms of verbal abuse. The same holds true after a separation with your ex. Asking for an apology or imploring for your ex to return is likely to be a fruitless endeavor because your ex is unlikely to be willing to listen or make a compromise at this time. You can completely avoid this lose-lose situation by choosing not to badger your ex.

You require time and room to organize your thoughts and emotions. You owe it to yourself to spend some time alone processing what just transpired, dealing with your emotions, and clearing your mind of negative thoughts. If you truly want to get back together with your ex, you must take the time to regain your calm and composed demeanor, free of wrath, rage, and other destructive emotions.

You need some alone time to pursue personal growth and other positive changes in your life. Utilize the no-contact period to reevaluate your goals and evolve into a better version of your former self. Keep in mind that you are doing this not only to demonstrate to your ex that you are in a better position than before, but also to strive for genuine intellectual and emotional development. During the no-contact period, there are a few activities that you may choose to pursue. These are examined in depth in the following chapter.

Your ex-partner needs time and space to sort out his or her emotions. Clearly, your ex requires the same amount of time to fully comprehend the recent events. It would be unrealistic to expect your ex to be willing to speak or make concessions in such a short period of time. Provide your ex with the necessary space. Above all else, respect his or her privacy.

Desperation and dependence are not attractive. When you exhibit an excessive propensity for possessiveness, you come across as somewhat frantic. Humans are hardwired to desire what they cannot have, so you are actually doing yourself a great injustice if you continue to pursue a conversation with someone who is not yet ready or willing to do so. The use of emotional coercion is also a major no-no. You want to be respected and adored, not pitied, at the end of the day.

The importance of enforcing a no-contact period and adhering to it regardless could not be emphasized enough. If you are disciplined enough to remain committed to this concept, avoiding all forms of communication with your ex will do marvels for you on a personal level and will be of great assistance as you attempt to regain your ex's love and affection.

How To Regain His Confidence

Are you the responsible party? Did the relationship terminate because he lost confidence in you? Have you made an error that you are aware of and would do anything to rectify in order to regain his trust? If you answered "yes" to any of these queries, the information in this chapter will be of assistance. The virtue of trust is that I believe it can be regained after being lost. You must realize that a man desires to feel as though he is the sole focus of his partner's attention. He desires to be completely secure in his relationship. In my opinion, it takes men longer to regain faith in a woman than it does for women to regain trust in a man. Therefore, if you wish to regain your ex-partner's trust, you must be patient. Realize that regaining his trust is unlikely to occur within the next week, next few months, or even the following year. However, keep in mind that if given the chance, it can be earned again.

One of the most essential aspects of regaining someone's trust is to be completely honest with yourself and with him. You must be willing to acknowledge and disclose any errors you may have committed. When attempting to regain someone's trust, you must not only be forthright about your past transgressions, but also be willing to be truthful in the future. I say this because, even if you acknowledge your mistakes and rectify the situation, any hesitation to be truthful about anything in the future can erode trust once more.

If you were accustomed to telling even white lies in your relationship, you must break this tendency. You should make it a priority to demonstrate to your ex that he has nothing to fear about if you two ever reconcile. Make it clear that you have nothing to conceal as his girlfriend or even as his friend. You will be well on your way to regaining his trust if you can combine opening up, admitting your errors, and eliminating lies with the fact that time heals all wounds.

When attempting to regain his trust, don't focus solely on demonstrating that you no longer lie or conceal things. Show him that you are an all-around decent person who genuinely cares about him. This can take his mind off of trusting you and allow him to appreciate you as an individual. I'm not suggesting you become a complete sap, but simply demonstrate that you care. If you go overboard with the niceness and eventually get him back, he will expect you to continue being overly nice, so if you don't want to be a complete suckup forever, don't be one now. Regaining his trust requires demonstrating that you have learned from your past errors and proceeding slowly.

Verify That He Is Worth It

It makes no difference how the relationship ended, who did what, or who was right and who was wrong. Before attempting to win back your ex, you must determine whether he is even worth winning back. It may require considerable effort on your part to regain your ex's affections. You must ensure that all of the effort you are expending will be worthwhile in the end. Ensure that you will be happy if you achieve your objective of repairing your relationship.

So many women have gone through hell to get their man back, only to place themselves back in a bad situation. If you wish to reunite with your ex-boyfriend, I assume it's because he was a positive influence in your life. If he didn't do that when you were together, you need to evaluate the situation carefully, even if the failed relationship was your responsibility.

Do not become so preoccupied with reuniting with your ex that you neglect his qualities as a boyfriend. This relates to the question I posed at the outset of the book, "Does he fulfill your relationship dreams?" If you answer this question honestly and determine that the answer is no, he is probably not worth pursuing. Please keep in mind this.

Do Not Sacrifice Your Joy To Win Him Back

If there is only one thing you take away from this book, let it be this. Under no circumstances should you sacrifice your pleasure to get your ex back. This is one of the worst acts one can do in their lifetime. In a relationship, there should be mutual happiness between all partners. In a relationship, it should not be solely about one person's wants and/or requirements. It is vital to bear in mind that it is not uncommon for a man to reunite with his ex-girlfriend in order to take advantage of her. Beware if you transform into the "I will do anything to get you back" girl. This attitude may result in the return of a man who believes he can stroll all over you and say and do whatever he wants. Even if your ex wasn't like this before, if you come across as entirely submissive, you're likely to end up in a miserable relationship that will leave you miserable, which you don't want, right?

I am not suggesting that you should not be willing to make sacrifices when necessary. I am merely stating that you should not yield so much that you are essentially forced to sacrifice your identity. Remember that your ex-boyfriend was once your boyfriend, which means he fell in love with who you were and who you are as an individual. If you have been following this guide, it should be fairly obvious at this point what sacrifices you may have to make. Make concessions that will benefit you both. Consider this: if you must completely alter who you are in order to win him back, he is probably not the appropriate man for you.

The Most Effective Method To Win Him Back

Okay, here we go. In this section, I will outline what I believe to be the most effective method for getting your ex-boyfriend back. Are you all set? It is for your confidence and happiness. This may sound easier than it is, particularly if you miss your ex terribly. I assure you that this method works, and I will explain why. Being confident and content is attractive. People enjoy being around confident and joyful individuals. When your ex observes that you are doing well and are generally content, he will want to be a part of that. Here's the positive aspect of this. You don't want a boyfriend who doesn't want to be with someone who is confident in themselves and content with their existence, do you?

You may still be thinking, "Yeah, that's nice, but I'm not confident or happy right now, which is normal." To overcome these negative emotions, however, you must consider the future and the large picture. The majority of individuals desire to be in a relationship in order to complete or enhance their satisfaction. However, the operative term here is happiness. This is exactly what you seek. Utilize this next piece of advice diligently. Imagine yourself in a happy, stable relationship with someone who desires to be with you whenever you are feeling depressed and missing your ex. Consider the feeling you will have on vacation with this person, when you marry this person, and when you establish a family with this person. Instead of focusing on the individual's visage, you should concentrate on the emotions evoked by their thoughts. You may need to ponder these thoughts once a day or one hundred times a day, but they will help you get through the day and eventually lead you to the professional and personal relationships you desire. I do believe that positive thoughts attract positive events into our existence. True self-assurance is one of the most attractive qualities a woman can possess. Never overlook that!

How to Get Your Ex to Sleep with You Once More

If you want to know How to Get Your Ex-Boyfriend to Sleep with You, there are a few tips you should remember. You must first determine why you want to cohabit with him. You cannot use 'I'm contrite' to win him back, and doing so will only exacerbate the situation. Your ex-boyfriend likely feels like the stereotypical angry ex who holds you responsible for the separation. Do not appeal to him. It is preferable to send him text messages or small gifts.

Understand Why You Desire To Sleep With Him

If your ex is still attempting to emotionally attach to you, it is highly likely that he wants to intercourse with you. He likely laments the intimacy of your relationship and desires to maintain it. While you may have moved on from him, he must still sense a connection to you. If he seems too distant, don't lose faith. There are multiple factors why he may be attempting to sleep with you.

Your ex-boyfriend's desire for intercourse may stem from a desire for love and appreciation, or he may be hoping to regain your affection. In any case, there are a number of indicators that could help you determine whether to sleep with him again. The length of time between your last intercourse and your breakup may have also contributed to your desire to have sex with your ex. Nevertheless, you should be honest with yourself about why you want to sleep with your ex-boyfriend. It may indicate a profound need for affection and appreciation.

It may be difficult to let go of the relationship, but it is essential to recognize that the past no longer requires your presence, whereas your future does. You should also realize that you are free to engage in sexual activity with your ex-boyfriend. The decision to move on is the most crucial step in the recovery process, despite the fact that letting go may feel terrifying. If you cannot let go of your ex, you should consider running away.

spend time recovering after a divorce

You are likely to be in a state of extreme emotion after a separation, which can cause you to make poor decisions and want to sleep with your ex again. In order to prevent such a scenario, set a no contact period. This period may last anywhere between two weeks and several months. During this time, strive to concentrate on your health and personal development. Seduction is analogous to dancing; one misstep can derail the entire performance.

Give yourself time to recover to avoid rekindling your relationship. Everyone has a different timeline for recovery, and it may not be healthy to attempt to adhere to a specific timetable. According to Dr. Sarah Bren, a psychologist based in Manhattan, "it is best to take your time recovering after a breakup in order to get your ex-boyfriend to sleep with you."

After a breakup, avoid showing symptoms of desperation or weakness. People are visual creatures, so it is improbable that your ex-boyfriend would want to see you acting as a doormat. Your ex-boyfriend will lose respect for you and the relationship will end in tears if you continually disclose your stomach. Instead, you should ensure that he feels cherished and safe.

Avoid begging him to sleep with you.

Although making love with your ex may temporarily resolve some issues, it is never a good idea to do so immediately after the breakup of your relationship. Your ex may be motivated more by delight than emotional connection. Furthermore, it is highly unlikely that he will want to sleep with you again. Don't waste time attempting to convince him to share a bed with you!

Making your ex feel like a victim by appealing with him is inappropriate. Begging diminishes your relationship and places all of the power in his hands. The ideal outcome would be for him to succumb to your pity, but that is not what you desire. Use subtle pressure to persuade him that he requires you. And avoid giving him the impression that you are asking him to make reparations and reconcile.

Do not beg your ex-girlfriend to let you sleep with her. This strategy is ineffective because males are territorial creatures, and you will only provoke him to want to fight you. He may be seeking to regain control and will do anything to achieve this. However, pleading will only make him appear weak and pitiful. And remember, you never know when he might return to you.

Text him insults.

The most effective method to persuade an ex-boyfriend to reignite the passion you shared prior to the breakup is to adopt his mindset. Remember your earliest romantic encounters? These were brimming with passion. During the first few weeks of every relationship, you attempt to impress your partner. To entice your ex to want to sleep with you again, you must recreate the previous atmosphere.

Your ex-boyfriend wants to sleep with you for a straightforward reason: he misses you and wants to reconnect. He desires to reconnect with you because he still laments the intimacy you shared. He is attempting to maintain your sexual connection even after the separation. If he were a male, he would want to sleep with you to avoid the emptiness he would experience if he severed ties with you.

Once the fire has been reignited, it is time to focus on communication. Try subliminally communicating with your ex. Send a message stating "No Communication." This message informs your ex that you are no longer required to communicate with or play a role in his life. By doing so, your ex will become perplexed and question whether you can win him back.

Do not exert pressure or act too cheaply.

Remember that intimacy is a two-way street if you wish for your ex-boyfriend to fall in love with you again. Men are not obligated to sleep with their fiancée, so they should not feel compelled or act opportunistically in order to do so. Be sincere and demonstrate that you appreciate spending time with him. Your genuine interest in him will delightfully surprise him, and he will want to see you again.

In terms of intimacy, males dislike being compelled to commit. In addition, males dislike being spoken to excessively about commitment or pressured to make a decision. They desire the excitement and closeness of love but have no interest in commitment discussions. Instead, maintain the least formal relationship feasible. This will increase his likelihood of committing to you.

Improve your flirtation skills when you meet.

Flirting involves more than just words. Body language and contact are significant indicators of interest. You can compliment your ex, but avoid being too evident. If you wish to adopt a more relaxed tone, try referencing an inside jest. Playing games with your ex will lighten the atmosphere and encourage conversation. There are a variety of games that you can play with your ex; experiment to determine which works best.

Reconnecting with your ex is the initial stage in rekindling a relationship. Beginning with casual conversation, gradually incorporate flirtation into the dialogue. Start with phone calls and text messages, then move on to in-person meetings. Your ex will eventually develop a stronger attraction to you. If this doesn't work, try changing the criteria so that your ex thinks more positively of you.

Create the impression that you are hanging out with your ex-boyfriend rather than a stranger. Avoid a "hello" or anything too obvious, such as asking for a refreshment. Instead, attempt to spend at least ten minutes with him. You can ask him out again or even invite him to a drink after a few minutes. However, avoid giving him any indications that you want to date him again.

Don't immediately yield to his demands.

While it may be alluring to reconcile, it's likely that your ex has his own reasons for not wanting to. He might be anxious about being apart from you, or he might have internal conflicts. Regardless of the cause, you should not immediately give in to your ex-boyfriend. Attempting to convince your ex to return to you will only drive him further away. Instead, you should concentrate on repairing the damage you've caused to the relationship and cease being selfish.

Your ex may still wish to see you, despite your sorrow. Attempting to win him back by pleading for additional time will only drive him further away. Your ex will find you less alluring if you appear desperate. Instead, demonstrate your strength and prevent him from taking advantage of you. This will also prevent him from engaging in manipulative behavior and give him the impression that you desire his return.

Activities For The Thirty-Day Period

Remember how you will implement the no contact rule for the next 30 days? Yes, but you're not just going to stay there and twiddle your thumbs during that time. No, you will work towards your objective of a new beginning in your relationship by focusing on making it better and the only variable you can influence, yourself!

This is an extremely important section that will offer you ideas and be of great assistance during the 30-day waiting period.

Reiterating the No Contact Period Rules:

-You may not contact, text, write, email, or Facebook your ex-boyfriend.

-You must avoid digging into your ex's existence in order to avoid obsessing and overthinking the situation.

-If your ex contacts you via email, phone, Facebook, or text message, you are not permitted to respond.

-Ignore anything your ex says about you, even if they are offensive remarks.

-If you violate your no contact rule (by communicating with him at all during the 30-day period), you must restart your 30-day no contact period.

Mental modifications you can concentrate on:

Immerse yourself in work - The best way to deal with this is to temporarily divert your attention, and what better method to do that than with work? However, you must be cautious not to lose yourself in your work and forget your primary objective. Remember that, in this instance, you should use work to prevent yourself from thinking about your ex.

Renew a hobby - This is essentially taking up a pastime that you used to enjoy but no longer have time for, such as golf, tennis, collecting, puzzles, photography, music, or hiking.

Sometimes your mind can't help but race with thoughts of your ex, and since you can't speak to him for 30 days, it may be a good idea to write them down in a journal or diary so that they remain conscious and not subconscious.

Have fun - If your peers invite you to go clubbing or partying, I recommend that you accept their invitation and enjoy yourself with them. In all honesty, time is the most effective method for getting over a breakup, but having fun is a close second.

Friends are a blessing, so reconnect with them. You can discuss your problems with them, and they will gladly listen and offer advice. You can rely on them to help you through difficult circumstances. But be cautious; do not allow them to convince you to call him before the no contact period expires.

Physical modifications you can make:

Who am I to dispute with the experts? I'm not a hair expert, but I know enough about men and have done enough research to conclude that this is an excellent strategy for looking good for your man.

Get in shape - There is no excuse or argument you can make to me that this won't completely alter your ex's perception of you, and not just physically, because it requires a great deal of mental fortitude to accomplish this. This is especially true if you are overweight and have been taking the escalator instead of the stairs. Nonetheless, if you enjoy staying in shape, don't let your breakup alter that. Keep doing you.

Change your diet - Once again, this is a fantastic way to feel better about yourself by simply replacing your old diet with a much healthier one. Observe how it forces you to do the opposite of sitting around all day consuming ice cream.

Update your wardrobe - I now give you permission to go shopping until you collapse! You can thank me when you are on the arm of your man.

Clean up your grin - No, I do not mean to smile more, although you should do so. I am referring to investigating the possibility of obtaining a new smile. If your smile is not what it once was, you should visit the dentist to have your teeth cleansed.

Take care of any skin issues you may have - If you have discoloration, excessive acne, or unwanted blemishes, you can have them treated by a professional or gradually over time. If you want them gone, you must set aside your vanity and treat them appropriately.

The Approach

You need a plan that you can execute in almost every aspect of your life, including bringing your boyfriend back. It just so happens that I have devised the most effective strategy for reclaiming your ex-boyfriend. I present "The Game Plan," a collection of cool psychological tactics that, if implemented correctly, will give you the best chance of regaining your ex's affections.

Step 1 is the initial contact text

When messaging your ex, avoid short responses such as "Hey," "Hi," and "What's up?"

(Explained in depth in the preceding chapter.)

Step 2: Enjoyable moments

If you have your ex's attention and an acceptable response, you can proceed to the next step. I will concede that you will have a much greater advantage if you have a lengthy history and, as a result, many wonderful memories. This aspect of appealing to your ex's emotive side may be a bit more difficult if your relationship was brief. However, this does not indicate a negative outcome; it merely suggests that you may need to be more inventive.

Big No-No's

This text is not intended to be a "booty call."

You cannot become enraged or upset.

-You shouldn't expect anything (manage their expectations). -This is not a cure-all for your entire relationship.

Do not request a meeting with your former.

The purpose of "remembering the good times" is to elicit thoughts of the relationship's more positive aspects. Therefore, you will need to be as upbeat and cheerful as possible.

Consider this: if you send these messages appropriately, you have a good chance of getting your ex to feel the same way you do, and they will begin to recall the good times you shared.

What Can I Say?

When you send him a text message, you will need to provide a great deal of specifics rather than relying on the possibility that he will understand the essence. Let's examine a few basic expressions to expand upon this point.

Example: "I'm currently at Gessen Park, and it reminds me of when I used to observe your football practices. Wish you were present!

Third Step: Using Jealousy

Utilizing your ex-boyfriend's envy to your advantage is one of the most effective strategies you can employ, according to all sources I've consulted.

Imagine a scenario in which a man wound up ending his 5-month relationship with a woman for an absurd reason. After three months of being single, the lady began dating a new man. Instantaneously, the man became envious, realized what he had, and desired her back. Until he saw her with another man, he didn't realize what he had.

This is the strength of envy.

Now, I am NOT suggesting that you begin a new relationship. However, you can still go on dates and leave hints in your ex's messages that you are meeting new people. The secret to success is NOT TO BE OBVIOUS. Do you believe that boasting that you are out with other men will help you advance in your relationship? No. There is an art to subtly incorporating these messages into your conversations, and I will teach you that art.

Creating envy in him via text message is quite simple.

Observe below how I did not indicate whether this acquaintance was male or female. You have just planted a seed of doubt in your ex-boyfriend's mind, causing him to question whether you watched a romantic movie with a friend or a date.

Message example: "I just saw (title of a romantic film) with a friend. It was an excellent film; I highly recommend it.

A message of the form "Hey, did I see you at?" is another common method for inciting envy. This idea was developed by one of my close friends, and I must say that it functions exceptionally well.

Message example: "Was that you I saw at (location) last night? You looked amazing!

Your ex-boyfriend is most likely thinking, "I wasn't at the pictures last night." This is ideal because he will continue to think about it and realize that you were interested in another man who was not him. Additionally, you are indirectly praising him. Aren't jealousy text messages extremely intriguing?

Fourth, the heart-to-heart

Okay, so let's take a step back and assess the current status of the game plan.

Step 1: You sent a first contact text message (and received a positive or impartial response while keeping the conversation brief).

Step 2: You initiated a genuine conversation with the "remembering the good times" text message (again, you controlled the conversation).

Step 3: You added a touch of jealously (you kept it subtle and got him to consider you as a potential girlfriend again).

After that, you will implement a number of small heart-to-heart conversations in various methods that will change your fortune for the better.

Important points to remember: -Avoid falling for the 'booty call' deception.

You cannot become enraged or upset.

-Don't have any expectations (manage them) -Don't attempt to remedy everything at once.

Do not request a meeting with your former.

-Always maintain a positive attitude.

Fifth step: the risk

This section focuses on taking a leap of confidence. Organizing a date with your ex-boyfriend for the first time since you broke up is significantly more essential. Relationship specialists have divergent opinions on how this should be carried out. In all likelihood, your ex-boyfriend has already offered to meet you IN PERSON if you've followed this guide's recommendations. However, if he didn't, don't worry; each circumstance is unique, and I have a plan designed specifically for you!

(Note: Only use 'The Risk' plan described below if he hasn't already offered to meet up and you perceive he's hesitant to make the first move toward a physical meeting.)

It's time to remove your gloves, women! NO MORE TEXTING! At least until the next section.

The Scheme

You will contact him with the intention of attending a modest gathering. The key to this is to not be aggressive or forceful. Your ex-boyfriend may be less receptive to meeting you in an inconvenient or ostentatious location.

Examples of acceptable meeting locations include coffee shops, restaurants, etc. (a lunch meeting is less formal than a supper meeting)

Guidelines for the call: -The phone conversation must appear harmless.

Plan your phone call for a time when you know your ex will be available to speak in private.

- You desire the phone call to be brief, upbeat, and pleasant.

- DO NOT recall any unpleasant memories from the past.

- Don't be frantic.

- Manage your expectations.

- Call no more than ONCE PER DAY, even if he doesn't answer.

- Don't leave a voicemail.

Two methods for making the call:

I did extensive research on this section and discovered that there are two distinct ways to make this essential phone call. The first method is "I was in the area," and the second is "a week beforehand." I don't have a preferred method, so I leave it up to you to decide which one to use.

First Strategy - I Was In The Neighborhood...

This method is risky and may not result in a meet-up invitation, but it allows you to try again later, whereas the method below it places your cards on the table. Okay, the operation of this is straightforward:

Your Message to Him: "Hey, Jake! I was in the area and thought it would be enjoyable to catch up. Are you interested in meeting at Starbucks?'

Again, this is hazardous because he has a greater likelihood of saying no. However, if you two were making significant progress via messaging and you believe he feels the same way about your current relationship as you do, the "I was in the area" method may work for you. The apparent benefit is the instantaneous date/meeting!

Strategy 2 - One Week In Advance

The week ahead procedure is exactly as it sounds. You call him a week beforehand to invite him out. This has the apparent benefit of allowing him to clear his schedule and make time for you. The only disadvantage, however, is that you are laying most of your cards on the table, making rejection an agonizing stab to the heart. Regarding rejection...

What to do if he rejects your proposal?

Avoid despair. Probably, he will say something like

"Uhh…. I'm not sure."

If so…

Simply chuckle a little and say, "Come on, it's just lunch" or "It's just coffee." Usually, the "I don't know" will be replaced with "okay." Put your doubts and concerns to rest.

If he continues to decline, do not despair. Even if you feel the urge to:

-Plead -Gain exasperation -Reiterate arguments -Attack him

Accept his refusal with grace, say farewell, and end the conversation on a positive note. This will increase his respect for you and leave the door open for future conversations.

Sixth step: the meeting

Yes, even for your mini-date/meet up/whatever you want to name it, there are rules. As stated previously, you want this gathering to be as informal as feasible. Don't arrange to meet over a nice dinner. I suggest a coffee date at Starbucks, where you can relax on the lounges and chairs and converse. Another great idea would be to take a stroll through your local park and converse or even have a picnic while doing so. The dates I've appreciated the most weren't extravagant or romantic; rather, it was simply when I was enjoying someone's company and walking around, without expectations and allowing things to flow organically.

Experts suggest that you go out for a beverage or something similar. Personally, I have no objections, but I would advise you to limit yourself to one drink. The last thing you want is to frighten your ex by declaring your eternal affection for him. The key is to do something that both of you will appreciate so that you can have fun and communicate.

Avoid excessive romanticism. Simply practice honest and transparent communication. Hopefully, your ex-boyfriend will want to see you again after the reunion. Then YOU'RE IN!

What should follow the date?

Okay, I just added this section based on my own dating experiences. I've heard that men like to hear how the date went, so to reassure them and get them thinking about the next time they'll see you, text something like: "How was the date?

Today was very enjoyable.

Women who take this action are always off to a good start. Good success!

Allowing One Another Space To Process Things

After a separation, both parties must give one another ample space to sort out their emotions and process what just transpired. It would be imprudent to initiate contact too soon, as the strong and potentially virulent emotions have not yet been mitigated by time and introspection. In addition to unhealed emotional traumas, one's sense of rationality may also be clouded by unpleasant memories. Therefore, it is prudent to take a step back, inhale deeply, and leave the other party alone for the time being.

The answer to the query of how much time is required before making contact depends on a variety of factors. For instance, it takes significantly longer for wounds to heal in a long-term relationship than in one that lasted only a few encounters. In determining the amount of time required as space, it is also crucial to consider the significance of the reason for the breakup. In general, trivial reasons are much easier to discuss than those that negate complex discussions.

Allowing her privacy

Nonetheless, this need for space must be respected at all costs, especially if you intend to gain your ex-girlfriend back. If you continue to harass her with phone calls, texts, and emails immediately after the separation, you will incur her ire. Instead of giving you her attention, she would likely exclude you entirely from her existence. Remember that if there are two things that can repel someone, it is desperation and neediness.

The general norm is to avoid all forms of physical contact. Due to the pervasiveness of online presence through social media networks and even mobile phones, it can be difficult to avoid encountering each other at some point. Do not delete her from your list of online acquaintances; doing so will be interpreted as a sign of bitterness and will lead your ex-girlfriend to believe that you no longer need her, which is obviously not the case.

Simulating ignorance

Similarly, if both of you operate within the same social circle, it is not out of the scope of possibility that you will meet. You need only be courteous and smile or say hello if you stumble into one another, but leave it at that. Refrain from conversing with her or remaining in her presence unnecessarily (and creepily). You wish to demonstrate that you are leaving her alone and do not intend to disturb her. In other words, allow her to possibly mourn you.

However, ignorance deception has its own limitations. You want to give her space, but you don't want to give her so much space that she can find a replacement for you. The following chapters will provide information on how to arouse her curiosity about you to the point where she will want you back.

3.Love is expressing regret

Therefore, between six weeks and two months have passed since the breakup. The most difficult part is over. You have invested in yourself and your own well-being and laid the necessary foundation.

It is likely that you are feeling calmer at this juncture. Your viewpoint is adjusting. Though you still mourn your ex intensely, you feel more empowered;

not only to live as you wish, but also to initiate the active phase of regaining your ex's affection.

Hopefully, over the course of the last few weeks, you have revisited the inventories you created at the outset of this process. You are acquiring a deeper understanding of the relationship. The portions that worked and those that did not. And the ways in which both partners contributed to or exacerbated the problematic aspects of the relationship.

You may believe that he bears the majority of responsibility. In this context, the term 'blame' is ineffective because blame is rarely a unilateral concept. Although one partner may have contributed more to the relationship's failure than the other, both partners were engaged in determining the relationship's course. As we have previously discussed, a tango requires two partners.

To get your ex back permanently–to get him back and keep him–a change in lifestyle is required. This guide is about investing in your health and emotional maturity in order to establish solid foundations for a long-lasting relationship. The ability to apologize for one's role in a problem is one of the most difficult aspects of maturation.

You might not be solely accountable. You may believe that the other partner contributed more to the problems in your relationship. However, apologizing for the role you did perform will not necessarily increase your chances of getting your ex back. It will increase your odds of retaining him permanently.

The third activity is the apology.

Launch Microsoft Word on your computer. Then, using the outlines you created in Activity #1, compose an apology letter to your ex for the ways in which you contributed to the negative emotional dynamic in your relationship.

It is not necessary that it be attractive or poetic. However, it is essential to get certain aspects right.

Remember that this is an apology above all else. No more, no less. Not a defense of yourself, not a debate, and not an assault on him. No begging or assurances that you will improve your behavior. Do not even mention the possibility of reconciliation at this time. You are simply apologizing for your role in the relationship's problems. Delete any additional errors that appear in your letter as you write.

Avoid a begging or desperate tone. Delete any queries that begin with

"Don't you think that you could have..." or "Couldn't we just..." The letter should not include any requests or demands.

The letter must be completely genuine. If you find yourself writing with anger or sarcasm, you are not yet prepared. Try again tomorrow after taking a bath, going for a stroll, or doing something to clear your mind.

The letter must focus on your conduct, not his. Do not dwell on the portions of his past that you believe he was responsible for.

The letter should not contain a defensive tone. If you find yourself writing phrases such as "I'm sorry about the time I did A, but I had no choice because you continued to do X, Y, and Z..." delete them. If you frequently find yourself composing defensive sentences, you are not yet prepared to write this letter.

Allow yourself a few additional days for your thoughts to resolve.

Make no demands. Make no requests. Do not discuss the future.

Write with composure and without excess emotion.

Grace is the central motif of this letter. In composing this letter, you are exhibiting elegance. Therefore, write simply and honestly, without expecting a response or even contrition. This letter is a comprehensive gesture in and of itself.

Simply sign off with something like, "I'm sorry for the inconvenience, and I hope you're doing well."

Rewrite the letter until you are satisfied, if necessary. Then, if desired, you can hand-copy it onto letter paper to add a personal flourish.

Put it in the mail. If you hand-deliver it, your ex may perceive you as pursuing him. Then dismiss it from your mind.

If your ex responds: Your ex could respond. He may even contact you to offer an apology in return. If so, receive his apology with grace. Do not make any additional accusations or passive-aggressive suggestions about his guilt. By apologizing, you place the past behind you. Do not bring them up again to cause him harm.

If your ex does not respond, you may never receive a response. That's alright. Attempt not to feel offended or resentful.

You are not writing him to request a response or a contrition. You are writing this letter as a therapeutic gesture for both you and him.

You desire change. You are not apologizing in an attempt to "win him back" or to sway his opinion. This letter is part of a longer-term effort on your part to become a more likable, mature, and fascinating individual.

"But what if...?"

As you read this, you may have several queries.

"But what if I'm not willing to apologize?" Perhaps you are so wounded by the breakup that you believe he should apologize. If you cannot see beyond the pain to the ways in which you contributed to the relationship's failure, you are not yet prepared to apologize.

That's alright. Take additional time if necessary. It is essential not to fake or impose emotion. This letter must be written from the heart.

However, if months pass and you still do not feel ready to apologize, this should serve as a red flag. Consider: If my relationship caused me such profound anguish and resentment, do I really want it back? Is my ex-boyfriend my soulmate?

If the response is negative, it is time to seek elsewhere. And that is without guilt.

"What if my ex reads the letter and concludes that I am a stalker?" It's improbable. If you've adhered to the plan, this is the only contact you should have had with him since the breakup. You waited a very considerate amount of time before contacting me again.

And this is why it is essential to strike the proper tone. Consult a reliable acquaintance. Request that they review the letter and strike out anything that appears imploring, demanding, or whiny. Request their honesty.

"Too much embarrassment prevents me from writing this letter; I'm too disturbed by my own errors to do so. Accepting responsibility for our own errors is a bitter pill to stomach. But if you want to get your ex back permanently, you will need to develop this habit.

This process involves establishing habits that will not only help you win back your ex, but also strengthen your ability to maintain the relationship and retain him for the long term. The ability to apologize when at fault, even partially, is essential for the renewal and survival of your relationship. And when you apologize with grace, you establish a relationship culture that encourages him to apologize for his mistakes.

Once you have honestly and openly documented the ways in which you were responsible, you will feel better.

Confronting your errors is the first step in managing and expunging your own guilt. Examine the written documentation of your actions. I'm sure they appeared larger and more menacing in your mind.

We are merely mortal. We make blunders. Typically, they are small and reversible.

To make restitution, however, we must identify our errors. We need to determine what went awry. And only then can we begin to demonstrate that we can perform better...

When we are fixated on an ex who is no longer in our lives, it is because we are fixated on the prospect of what could have been.

It is equally absurd to concentrate solely in the past or the future. In both instances, we have little or no control, as we can only influence the present moment.

You must let go of what might have been and courageously confront reality without the person you might have expected to be by your side.

Obviously, this requires you to be courageous, to sit down and create a recovery plan, to avoid the blame game by any means necessary, and to absolve yourself for any role you may have played or decision you may have made that led to this moment.

It is possible to get over an ex, but you must put forth effort and become accustomed to the discipline of letting go.

In the following pages, we'll delve a bit deeper into the topic of getting over an ex.

Come with me to the next page, where I once again invite Jane to tell you (in her own words) some of the things she tried that worked for her and how her experiences aligned with the scientific consensus on what helps people recover from a breakup.

Science Identifies Proven Methods For Overcoming Breakups

1. I fueled my body with nutritious food and exercise.

Grace Larson, a researcher at Northwestern University, stated, "It is essential to establish healthful physical rhythms after a breakup. She stated that breakups wreak havoc on our daily routines. To combat this chaos and disorganization, it is even more essential to eat regularly. It is more essential to ensure that you get enough sleep. Even more essential is to establish a new, consistent schedule for exercising.

The farmers market became a staple of the weekend. Together with my sisters and aunt, I went shopping and purchased chilled lemonade, ripe orchard apples, lush greens, and miniature summer squash.

I satiated my body's needs. I plotted out meals. I brewed numerous cups of green tea and French press coffee. I completely indulged myself.

Visiting the farmers market and adopting a mindset of self-indulgence regarding food was so enjoyable. But returning home and realizing I would have to consume these bounties alone wasn't so bad.

The greatest part is that my efforts to be kind to my body extended beyond food. I purchased a novice yoga pass at a nearby studio, and the entire experience was fantastic.

I slowly inhaled, trembled, and stretched while repeating the mantra, "I am the only person on my mat," several times. The practice of yoga became a means for me to become physically and mentally strong. It involved caring for myself and recovering from emotional trauma.

It enabled me to recognize how I was harming myself without engaging in the harmful behavior. Indeed, it was magnificent.

I left the studio feeling strong, complete, and at peace. Even if the sensation lasted less than 30 minutes per day, those 30 minutes were exquisite.

In addition to my yoga practices, I joined a gym near my house and began attending group exercise courses.

My ex was a personal trainer and a football player; he was powerful, confident around other athletes, and physically imposing.

I was clumsy, gym-phobic, and curvy, and I preferred to exercise in the safety and seclusion of my living room. I had declined each of my ex's invitations to the gym.

Currently, I have attended cycling classes and a gym boot camp. I engaged a personal trainer and devised a strategy to achieve my fitness objectives. I supplemented my gym sessions with rehearsals for the show's choreography and lengthy walks. I started to observe progress. When I lacked the motivation to exercise, I granted myself forgiveness.

Breakups are genuinely awful. They occasionally necessitate Netflix binges and Chinese takeout (additional duck sauce and the largest order of lomein possible, please).

My advancement was not swift. I didn't go vegan. However, the gym trainers recognize me, and a few even know my name. That is noteworthy.

If you choose to use food to contend with a breakup, you should do so with a friend. Eating kale by yourself and attempting to be joyful is a miserable experience.

In addition, it is tempting to indulge in excessive quantities of sweets and junk food.

DO NOT! DO NOT!!

DO NOT!!!

You will feel nauseous and crampy, and you don't want to further tax your body, which is already coping with a severe emotional setback.

As for the exercise component, there will be times when you consider the gym and you simply cannot go. On such days, you may feel worthless, lazy, or as though nobody will ever find you alluring again. Forgive yourself, rest, and nurture your body in alternative ways.

Take a bath containing various essential oils. Spend the night giving yourself a pedicure and moisturizing your legs. Walk for a considerable distance through the park and practice mindful respiration. You are not required to sweat every day, but you must be kind to yourself daily.

I reconnected with former companions.

According to Grace Larson, "breakups disrupt what psychologists term our "attachment systems."

"In the same way that a neonate relies on their primary caregiver or mother to comfort them, adults still have a strong need to form close bonds with another individual. And typically, there is a transition from childhood to adulthood; your attachment bond is with your father or mother, grandparents, or a close caregiver. As one enters adolescence, the attachment bond becomes one's dearest and most intimate companions. Then, as adults, our primary attachment will likely be to a romantic partner."

Larson posed the following question: "What happens after a breakup, when your partner is no longer your primary attachment?"

Many individuals reattach themselves to those individuals who, at an earlier period in their lives, served as their primary attachment.

Your attachment to close friends, parents, and even an ex-lover may return.

My closest female companions reside in Massachusetts and Maine. Prior to our breakup, my relationship with Michael consumed the majority of my time. As I basked in the ecstasy of a new relationship, I abandoned my past lovers.

After the separation, we were able to reestablish contact. I spent weekend after weekend taking long drives to binge-watch Netflix, whine, weep, cuddle, and verbally process my sorrow with my friends.

I gave the women in my life precedence. I spent many hours on the phone reconnecting with individuals with whom I had lost touch. There is nothing quite like being barefoot on your best friend's sofa with a glass of red wine and a box of tissues to make you feel at home.

These companions (ladies) reminded me that there were aspects of my past that had been unburdened by the breakup, or possibly even strengthened.

On multiple occasions, Happiness accompanied me on lengthy walks with her dog while we sipped mimosas over brunch. She anchored me to my most compassionate self. She consistently emphasized that I was still (and had always been) lovable.

Rosemary, or as I affectionately call her, Rosie, pushed me out of my comfort zone. I was taken rock climbing and to Walden Pond by her. She assisted me in commemorating my independence. She guided me through asking my ex to return my belongings.

Rosie and happiness helped me reconstruct the foundation of my strongest, happiest, and present self.

They served as a reminder that all was not lost.

If you are going through a breakup and reside far from your best friends, it may be more difficult to use these visits as a coping mechanism.

Therefore, communicate with them through ZOOM, SKYPE, and FaceTime. Plan your phone conversations in advance. Ensure that you can hear their voices.

Additionally, it can be difficult to remember that your peers have other responsibilities, such as jobs, relationships, and social lives, when you're experiencing heartbreak.

Therefore, when they are unavailable, remind yourself that it is not because they do not wish to assist you in feeling better.

There is no way to pour from an empty tumbler. Your most ardent supporters still require rest between cuddle sessions. It is not because they lack concern. Because they want to provide optimal care for you and themselves.

I barred my ex on all social media platforms.

When I asked Larson about this behavior, she cited the research of Leah

LeFebvre, a University of Wyoming professor who studies courtship and relationships.

Larson explained to me, "LeFebvre and her colleagues would refer to this as 'impression management' if you posted glitzy photographs as evidence of your thrilling new life. In contrast, they view barring or unfriending an ex as part of the access-reduction strategy."

He continued, "Researchers contend that they are both components of the process of dictating the storyline of the breakup ("I'm the victor in this breakup!"). These methods serve to demonstrate — to your ex, to yourself, and to anyone else observing — that you are independent and thriving in the aftermath of the breakup.

I am an avid Instagram user, Facebook stalker, Snapchat user, and social media devotee in general.

Immediate poison during the separation was this trait. I was ecstatic to be able to flaunt my new life and happiness, but a single update from my ex would leave me perplexed, depressed, and missing everything about him.

The afternoon he began posting pictures of himself with other women, I felt furious, sick, and betrayed. Instead of giving up the minor solace my social media accounts provided, I blocked him.

The blocking was indeed a very intelligent move. Not only did it prevent me from seeing any potentially heart-wrenching posts (from my ex), but it also prevented me from posting unnecessary fluff in an effort to make my life appear thrilling and rewarding in case my ex decided to view my profiles.

In actuality, my life is thrilling and rewarding, and letting go of the need to prove it has helped me participate in and appreciate it.

DOWNSIDES: It is very difficult to be unable to observe your ex's activities. When you are accustomed to being a part of someone's daily life — when you care about their success, their happiness, and whether they are achieving their objectives — the abrupt disconnect caused by the removal of social media can be overwhelming.

I can assure you, however, that it is beneficial in the long term.

You cannot dwell on the possibility that they are seeing other persons. You cannot examine all of their newly-added acquaintances or determine who likes their photos.

The pain of ignorance is significantly less painful than the pain of incessant obsession.

Trust me!

I devoted myself to my profession and career.

Larson stated, "Heartbreaks (or Breakups) cause you to feel helpless. They strip away your autonomy. Therefore, not only will you feel more attractive and valuable if you're killing it in your career, but it's also an area over which you have complete control."

Although the breakup hurt my emotions, it helped me solidify my professional goals and career.

Since the separation, I've been offered two competitive fellowship positions at the Centers for Disease Control and Prevention and in public health.

I am motivated to prepare for the graduate and law school entrance exams. And I have been able to focus on my work without interruptions.

The freedom of not having to consider another person's ambitions has been a saving grace for my self-love, as I have ardently pursued my goals.

I accepted a new position with a higher title and returned to a field that I am passionate about (prevention of gender-based violence).

At the age of 22, I gave my first lecture to university students on sex trafficking and sexual violence during conflict as violations of human rights.

I have submitted presentation proposals to three academic conferences, co-authored a chapter on the prevention of sexual violence, and authored multiple papers. I joined the Toastmasters public speaking club, honed my rhetorical abilities, and investigated opportunities in political journalism.

In conclusion, despite and because of the sorrow, I have succeeded. I have learned to never underestimate the strength of a woman in love or a woman who has recently been out of it.

There are no negative aspects here!

I downloaded Tinder and began dating casually again. According to Brian Boutwell, "dating after a breakup is a good idea because it's almost guaranteed to result in one of two outcomes: It will make you realize there are other fish in the sea, and therefore help you get over your ex, or it will inspire you to see the good things about your old relationship, and thus lead you to decide to get back together."

In both cases, there is the potential for an evolutionary payoff, he continued. You may either reunite with your former partner or acquire a new, perhaps more prospective partner.

This was the most terrifying aspect of my post-breakup revolution. After Michael and I broke up, I resolved to not have a serious relationship for at least a year.

He was nonetheless the last person I had kissed. The last person with whom I had shared a bed. The last person who had touched my tresses and (always, always) warmed my cold toes.

When I considered flirtation and closeness, I immediately thought of him. It rendered dating an absolute nightmare, which is precisely why I (re)downloaded Tinder and began communicating with new individuals.

I initially felt guilty and dishonest, as if I had betrayed my ex or made false promises to these new partners. However, after a few weeks I met some amazing individuals.

I went out for coffee and lunch and met warm, accomplished, ambitious, affectionate, and brilliant men and women who reminded me that I was desirable, intelligent, and charming.

These individuals treated me as if I were intriguing, and so I felt.

DOWNSIDES: You will feel bewildered. You will experience remorse. You will experience self-doubt. You may feel contemptible, humiliated, or filthy. You may feel as though you are exploiting others. You may experience dishonesty.

Not everyone is cut out for dating again after a breakup, particularly so soon after the breakup. (In truth, it is not recommended).

Additionally, you should not have sex with a new partner after a breakup, particularly so soon after the breakup.

Pay attention to your body and impulses. If you feel uncomfortable or gross during a date, it is acceptable to cut it short, return home, take a bath, and listen to a decent song such as "Bethel" until you feel comfortable again.

These were the measures that Jane chose to take in order to feel the most empowered and comforted during the heartbreak.

This does not mean that Jane is entirely over it. It requires patience.

I'm not sure there is such a thing as being "over it" all at once when you genuinely love someone.

I am confident, however, that you will regain your power and contentment with time. Your existence will feel gloriously like your own, affording you the chance to learn more about yourself.

People are drawn to those who enjoy the life they are leading.

Once you are able to take charge of your life and happiness, and are able to take an objective look at the situation and properly analyze the situation with your ex, and only then, are you suitable to enter the dating landscape – again.

How do you plan for the future?

Take The Initiative

You have already arranged a date. You have summoned your ex, and he or she is aware of your desire to meet. However, despite the fact that things are going well thus far, there are still a few days between now and your appointment, during which anything can regrettably occur. Instead of simply waiting for the day of the appointment, get things moving, but do so "undercover" (so that your ex does not discover your plans).

Depending on the scenarios presented, you will find below a variety of invitations to your ex to seriously consider what you have to say.

-Let down your guard: This means that regardless of whether your ex attempts to contact you before the appointment, you should be cordial and sociable. Don't be overly reticent. For example, if your ex calls you the next day after your initial phone contact and says, "Hey! Yesterday's conversation was fantastic, how are you? I trust I am not disturbing? At this very moment, you may begin to panic and wonder, What should I do? Well, play along and respond with an inviting tone; after all, you must place all the odds in your favor. Consequently, you can respond as follows: I enjoyed it as well, I look forward to seeing you on X day as opposed to certainly, certainly I did as wellSee you on X day which comes across as rude and rushed to end the conversation.

-Take the temperature: You can also relax your vigilance by initiating a call to your ex to, in a sense, "take the temperature." Taking the temperature means determining whether or not your ex is enthusiastic about meeting you later in the week. Call him/her and inquire about the status of everything. Begin the conversation normally with greetings, and then say, "it felt good to talk to you after all this time" to gauge his or her reaction (remember, you are taking the temperature to determine if you need to do more convincing before your "date"). If your ex sounds enthusiastic and anxious to speak with you, continue the conversation, make a few jokes (but not too many), and keep the conversation moving. Spend at least 10 to 15 minutes; it will be like giving a child a piece of his beloved cookie and then making him work for the remainder. When you proceed in this manner, you are provoking his/her curiosity, and your ex will undoubtedly come to meet you on this day, despite having better things to do.

-Conduct research to formulate your final strategy: Another thing you can do prior to the date is to conduct a little research with your ex's peers and acquaintances with whom you have maintained contact. Ask two or three individuals you both know who you believe can provide interesting information, such as: Who is he/she seeing? Is he content with his life? Has he or she mentioned you during their conversations? This is an essential step because it will indicate what you should or should not say to your ex later in the week. For instance, if a friend informs you during your investigation that your ex is in and out of relationships, this is an indication that he is currently emotionally unstable. Therefore, if you want him/her back, you'll need to add that special something that will make him commit or believe in the relationship, such as joint initiatives, greater trust, etc. Again, if that acquaintance informs you that your ex-boyfriend is about to launch a business, this gives you insight into his state of mind and suggests that he will be more receptive to a relationship in which he is motivated and not confronted with nonsense.

So, go ahead and jot down whatever information you deem essential and that will help you develop a better approach towards your ex, as you wouldn't want to sound off when you speak to him/her; for instance, if he/she recently lost a family member, you shouldn't focus your conversation solely on happiness and partying while the other person (your ex) is grieving. Get as much information as possible to determine his or her current state of mind.

-Be strategic and categorical: Now, let's discuss your conversational abilities. It's true that we're discussing your ex, and you must be thinking that you know him/her well enough that you don't need advice on how to approach him/her. In this respect, you are completely incorrect. He/she may have been your partner at one point in your life, but if he/she is now your ex, it indicates that something went awry, so you are likely not so adept at coping with him/her. We are not attempting to cast aspersions here (that is not our intention), but we do want to draw your attention to one thing: Now that you have decided to get him/her back, you will need to demonstrate your future ambitions with him/her in the next few days. You won't go there and start blurting out everything that's on your mind, and if the other person doesn't understand why you're nervous, that's alright; he or she will understand that you still have feelings for him or her. And it should be acceptable if the relationship is mutual. However, what if it is not? Therefore, you should take precautions. Be prudent and strategic by avoiding risk. You should jump in there, knowing that you adore this person very much and that it makes you nervous, but you don't want to make him/her run away (as previously stated, you must be aware of his/her state of mind). So, play it 50/50. You can have the nervous laugh and the sparkles in your eyes when you see him/her, but when you engage in conversation with him/her, you should act as if you are talking to your best friend, meaning that you should not explicitly imply that you want to get back together immediately. You must keep him/her speculating, provide a few hints here and there, and make sure you don't immediately get to the point. For instance, you could have him/her speak about him/herself first, and then 20 minutes later, you could bring up an old happy memory (in his/her mind, he/she will be thinking, "Wow! Why does she/he bring it up?). Then, a short time later, you can say something like, "I remember you've always wanted to be..." and then ask, "Are you still?" There, you are delving deeper and deeper into personal details. Utilize these strategic inquiries throughout the date to prepare your date (with hints) for when you will reveal your true intentions.

Here is a list of guidelines to help you remain strategic and objective throughout your date:

-Don¡¦t let your emotions take over. Again, avoid turning a sound strategy into a disgrace. Maintain your composure; you miss your ex and it pains sometimes, but having everything planned will prevent you from being automatically rejected by him/her and will also help you mature (be more responsible).

-Make your ex feel at ease; after all, you're the one who reintroduced him or her into your life; he or she could have chosen to do something else instead of meeting you; therefore, please avoid bringing up unpleasant recollections. This will squander both of your and his/her time. If you want to start over, take the positive aspects of your previous relationship and discard the negative ones (for the sake of reuniting).

-Speak from the heart and get straight to the point by bringing up recollections that you know will make him or her smile. This will reawaken something deeply dormant within him/her as a result of your absence, and it may help you easily reconquer him/her.

-Do not appear to be too harassing, unwind. If you don¡¦t; you will not get anything here. And seriously, your first appointment is just to let your ex know how you feel; you still have a lot of work to do, so take it easy, one day at a time, and you'll undoubtedly get what you want.

Put forth your utmost effort:

Now, it is essential to emphasize an essential point: your attitude. It cannot be stated enough that dealing with individuals, even a lover you believe you know by heart, is never simple. Therefore, you must fight with all your might, and who knows, maybe that's what your ex has always expected from you: more tenacity and enthusiasm in your endeavors.

What we mean is that rather than telling yourself You should not say, "Oh well, I have a plan, and he/she agreed to meet me; after that, whatever happens, happens"; instead, you should act as if you truly desire this.

First, ensure that you are prepared for anything. Consider the occurrence of an unpredictable event as a challenge that you can overcome. If, for example, your ex is seeing someone else, act as if it was an error and that he or she should choose you instead. Use whatever means necessary to persuade him/her. Perhaps you are the perfect person for him or her. Therefore, if you learn before the meeting that he or she may be in a relationship, be prepared to take control by being present, amusing, open, and a good listener. Take your partner back and give him or her what you believe he or she is not receiving from the other person.

Second, respond to any questions (if any) that your ex may pose. Remember that you are bringing a new spirit and vitality with you. Don't bring back the old "vibes" where you were so comfortable with where the relationship was that you neglected to pay attention to certain details, such as giving him/her occasional gifts, taking him/her out, or again complimenting him/her when he/she has lost weight or changed his/her hairstyle. Such circumstances may have been too irritating for the other person and contributed to your separation. This time, demonstrate your desire to do your best by responding to his/her questions. Consequently, you can reassure him/her.

Finally, you must strive for your relationship by being authentic. Be you! This is what attracted your ex to you in the first place, and if you have a self-esteem problem, now is the time to demonstrate that you possess character when you choose to. The true secret is that you will never get your spouse back if you pretend to be someone else. If you are not a sexual symbol, you are not a sex symbol. 365 days a year, don't even attempt to compel yourself down that path. Alternatively, if you attracted that person because you appeared to be in touch with your sensuality, don't attempt to be a "good girl." Simply be yourself and accept yourself.

Say the following phrases to boost your confidence: -He/she used to like me for who I was; otherwise, he/she would never have given me a second glance.

When he/she said he/she loved me, he/she meant that he/she loved me as I was.

-We broke up because I or he/she was unable to compromise, but that does not imply that I am incapable of or unwilling to do so in the future.

-Why wouldn't I do it again if I've already done it once?

You're here to persuade someone to give you a second chance, so put up your best effort and use your personality while doing so. Ultimately, you're trying to convince someone to give you a second chance.

The Appointment

Now that you've prepared for the past week, it's time to "get it right" for the big day that will determine whether or not you get your ex back. This is the first day that you will see each other again face to face, so you must make a decent impression (if not a perfect one). Consider this date to be the day you will re-enter your ex's consciousness; he should leave the date (or appointment) with the thought, "What if we gave it another shot?"

Mixing simplicity with pragmatism is an effective method to make the appointment easier for you.

Avoid dressing to impress.

People frequently make this error. Women apply excessive amounts of makeup and don their favorite lingerie, and then they consider using sex to win back their ex. Men exaggerate it by wearing excessively strong Eau de cologne, an excessive amount of jewelry, or a hairstyle reminiscent of a 1930s Hollywood actor. If your plan includes extravagant spending, abandon it. Be straightforward, and you know why? You must ensure that your ex is more concerned with your message and behavior than with your appearance, so avoid dressing to impress. Wear instead anything that is basic, clean, and elegant. Not too much, but not too little either; just the perfect amount. It should be the same with your perfume; you want to be comfortable and confident, so don't wear something that smells like it could harm a fly, and don't apply your makeup as if you're going out to a club.

Remember that your first impression is everything. Here are some tips to help you navigate that day:

-Consider, "What should he/she think of me?"That I want to immediately invite him/her to my room with this outfit?Will he/she regard me seriously while attired in this manner? Will he/she cancel the appointment because I will appear to be a fool?¡"

If you answered yes to any of these queries, you should reconsider your outfit choice.

The final step is to avoid being late, as it is common knowledge that choosing an attire for a romantic date can consume a great deal of time. Therefore, complete the entire procedure and prepare everything the day before your date.

Now is the time to get serious, as you are about to arrive at your appointment. Ensure that you arrive before your ex. If you arrive late, he or she may interpret your tardiness negatively, label you a failure, and cut the meeting short. Therefore, ensure that you arrive 15 minutes before the scheduled appointment time.

Now let's get to the heart of the matter: The engagement. You are finally within a few hours of reigniting his/her interest in you. Now is the time to put everything you've learned this week into practice.

Throughout the duration of the appointment, it is essential to keep in mind that although you must be yourself, relaxed, and employ persuasion techniques to convince your ex, you must also convince him or her to consider you seriously. One method to accomplish this is to look your ex in the eye when speaking with him/her and when he/she addresses you. This eye contact speaks louder than words and has the added benefit of creating the impression that you are telling the truth, thereby enhancing the gravity of the situation.

If you are anxious, periodically shift your shoulders back and breathe as slowly as possible.

When seated, adopt a comfortable position that allows you to communicate effectively. It means that if your legs are too short and you have a bit of a stomach, you shouldn't cross them. Do not take the chance of demonstrating that you lack control of the situation, as this will result in a loss of points. Because you initiated the meeting, you should maintain your composure at all times.

Now, let's discuss the discourse or language.

Okay, let's begin with the first sighting, which occurs when you see your ex arrive and he or she joins you. Smile at him or her; this should be effortless.

Next, express gratitude for attending. It would have been disastrous if he/she hadn't shown up, so that's the least you can do. Overall, during the engagement, you should act as if you were hosting someone (but not too much). It implies that if you are on a date in a restaurant, you should suggest a dish (especially if your companion is hesitating) with charm and courtesy. This type of attention will make him or her feel spoiled and special, which is excellent because he or she is likely lacking it in his or her life at the moment. And since he/she has already spent time with you, this additional attention will prompt rapid recall of all the good times you've shared together.

If you chose a park or other open space, be reasonable and have all snacks and beverages with you or available before your guest arrives. This is also romantic and possibly distinct from what he or she is accustomed to on a daily basis. Ensure that exposing someone to a new environment on occasion is always a positive experience.

During the few hours you have together, the conversation should focus on both of you. To get it going, ask inquiries. The queries you must ask must focus on weighty topics, such as personal interests. The fact that you know each other should make it easy for you to pose any question, but don't go overboard, as this is not an interrogation. Ask inquiries that you know will yield answers that will be useful in the future. Therefore, you should collect as much information as possible to determine whether you'll need to exert more effort than you anticipated or whether his/her life has changed since the last time you saw your ex. Remember that we've stated that everything must be strategic, so ask him/her personal inquiries (he/she won't mind since you were once lovers).

This should continue for the first thirty to forty minutes of the date. Then, recall recollections (choose one or two that you know will make him/her blush). If, during the first 30 to 40 minutes of your conversation, your ex has said something like, "Uh, I haven't met anyone serious yet" or "My life is more about work, I don't really care about the rest," then feel free to bring up a "great memory" so he or she remembers how special your relationship was. Say it as you would to a friend who is desperate for a "beautiful story." This is because you must immediately enter his/her mind. Consider it as if you were bidding against other individuals, and yours should be the winning bid. Your ex must know that he/she is receiving the best deal of his/her existence today.

This brief "story-telling" phase will conclude (certainly) with the two of you laughing or making remarks, indicating that you share some things (good memories). Enjoy the moment, and then explain why you wanted to meet with this person on this particular day.

Take his/her hand (as if making a declaration of love) and say, "I want us to give it a try." Then, pause and wait for his/her response. If he/she says, "Wow, I need to think about this," which he/she undoubtedly will, then you should respond with "I'll have to think about it." Assure him/her that you will not haste and that you will take things one step at a time. Then, drop the sealing argument "I've realized how much you helped me stay focused, and I've realized that only you could provide me with the type of stability I required." This is an uplifting sealing argument because you are elevating the opposing party. It is normal for individuals to be hesitant or speechless when their ex reveals that he or she still loves them. Reassure the individual, as demonstrated above, that the task can be accomplished together, step by step.

After your declaration, you will notice an immediate closeness because your ex may be pleased that you have returned. Likewise, he/she likely desired to contact you but was unable to do so. Alternatively, there will be some tension. The tension in this situation has nothing to do with anger; rather, it stems from the other person's realization that he or she may still have affections for you. Because your ex-partner showed up, you can rest assured that he or she still cares about you.

No matter what occurs, continue to reassure the person with phrases such as "there's no need to be embarrassed, it's me." Give the individual compliments such as "you look beautiful/nice tonight" or crack a jest such as "you look beautiful/nice tonight, did you do all this for me?" Wow!¡" Reassuring someone or making a jest makes them feel more at ease and natural around you, because they recognize that you are fostering this disposition through your conversation.

Now, the evening has gone according to plan because you've executed all of your strategies. It is now time to return home and separate. In an effort to leave your ex with a favorable impression of you, you must ensure that this final moment is handled with the same courtesy. This implies that you should pay the bill (dinner is on the house, remember), be a gentleman or lady, and invite your visitor to depart immediately. Do so with courtesy and a smile, regardless of how your ex responded to your invitation to reconcile (whether he seemed pleased or hesitant). Always keep in mind that the greatest thing is that he/she came tonight and that you shouldn't rush things (there will be other opportunities to have him/her in your pocket).

If your guest lacks a vehicle, offer to send him or her off. Again, this is an opportunity to demonstrate your concern. Ensure that, on the way back to his or her residence, you maintain a small conversation, such as, "What are your plans for tomorrow?" Work? or something like I suppose tomorrow we'll return to our routine, and engage something around it, but do so in a way that won't make you sound odd or monotonous. Be natural, as if you genuinely desire to discuss the topic.

If your guest lacks a vehicle, offer to summon a taxi for them (at your expense).

Regardless of the outcome of the appointment, you should say goodbye to your ex with an embrace or a peck on the cheek. Do not request a kiss on the lips, as this is inappropriate and could result in an immediate rejection because it is untimely, makes you appear frantic, and suggests that you are seeking sexual contact. Even if your ex appears to be collecting a final cup of coffee and invites you in, you should decline. You will score some points if you are strong, serious, and immensely attractive, as you are aware that people like what is difficult to obtain, including an ex-lover.

Consequently, an embrace or a peck on the cheek suffice.

Congratulations, you have successfully survived the night. You have surmounted apprehension, boredom, a lack of conversation, and, most importantly, being under too much pressure to initiate a sexual encounter.

Your ex-partner is undoubtedly recalling how solid the relationship was and is possibly weighing the options of giving you a second opportunity.

Let us now proceed to the next phase.

When Relationships Fail As A Result Of Other Factors

What happens if you've taken all the necessary steps to reunite with your ex, but he or she continues to avoid you?

There are instances in which relationships fail for no evident reason. Even if you believed things were going well, your ex may have decided to stop communicating with you, stop responding to your communications, and withdraw from the relationship as if you were never there.

The person who has been ostracized frequently believes they have done nothing wrong, whereas the person who has completely withdrew may have very distinct ideas about the relationship's initial trajectory.

In fact, a hormone that is quite similar to that which is secreted by those who fell in love may also be produced by those who have been shunned. This may further alienate your partner. The most effective strategy is to give them some space before confronting them.

Having OCD (Obsessive-Compulsive Disorder)

This is one reason why individuals in love are unable to concentrate at work, eat, sleep, or think about anything other than their partner.

Obviously, just because you feel a certain way does not imply that your partner felt the same way at the same time. Similar to how not everyone becomes famished at the same time, not everyone experiences the same emotions at the same time.

The unfortunate aspect of this is that occasionally one of the individuals in the relationship may contemplate taking the relationship to the next level. They will take some time to consider what will occur as the relationship progresses beyond the dating phase and will envision numerous scenarios.

This can lead one individual to believe that the connection is deeper than it actually is, whereas the other individual may simply be attempting to comprehend their own sentiments. This is occasionally called a "instant relationship." While one partner is in full relationship mode and wondering why the other partner isn't reciprocating, the other partner believes they are still courting.

In this situation, the worst mistake a person can make is to attempt to convince their partner that they should be together or that they are madly in love with them. Men may want to slow down or even depart when they observe women behaving in this manner because they are perplexed. Because they perceive their companion to be dependent and hopeless, they may occasionally distance themselves or even completely withdraw. Males are completely repulsed by a woman's desperation and insecurity.

Many men are guilty of treating the women they admire in precisely the same fashion. He can attempt to persuade her that he adores her more than any other man and is therefore the superior choice. These situations are problematic because it is difficult for them to comprehend that what they are doing is improper and a poor strategy for gaining someone's favor.

To determine the answer, contemplate the initial step.

Returning to the beginning of the relationship is almost always the key to regaining your ex's affection.

When you first met your significant other, how did they behave? More importantly, how did you conduct yourself when you first began dating?

You were likely both acting appropriately and treating one another with respect. You both work very hard to make the other person pleased. In addition, both of you would have been motivated to make a good impression on the other and would have overlooked any minor personality or behavioral defects. Consider your most recent exchange with your ex. Were you two interacting with one another effectively? Or did you disagree, feel tense, angry, or apprehensive over the other person's thoughts?

If you and your ex had difficulty getting along, the image of you in his or her mind is likely one of you fighting, being sad, crying, and being anxious about the future of your relationship. In this circumstance, it is impossible to conceive of a bright and cheerful future for the group. Instead, they're probably contemplating how to meet someone who is more similar to the first impression they had of you.

Yes, the individual that you were when we first met. When you first met, he or she fell in love with the optimistic, self-confident, ebullient, and independent person you were. When he or she was in your presence, you would have made him or her feel pleased and have them pondering when you would find time in your busy schedule to visit them again. What changed then?

Possible Errors in Your Attempts to Win Your Ex Back

Are you culpable of begging your ex to reconcile even after they have ended the relationship? Yes, despite the fact that your heart is breaking, you know that this is the person with whom you were meant to spend the remainder of your life. But does your ex share your sentiments?

If you have attempted to persuade your ex that you are the one for them by calling, messaging, emailing, or sending messages, you may be alienating them further. The problem with your frequent contact attempts is that your ex may perceive them as a sign of your desperation. Nobody relishes being desperate, male or female. It emanates insecurity and clinginess, which are extremely undesirable traits in any individual.

The confidence of the opposite gender is extremely alluring to both men and women. When a person exudes confidence, understands what they want, and is not reliant on others to make it happen, they are extremely attractive.

A person who suddenly determines that the only way they can be happy is by clinging to you is, however, suddenly unattractive. Keep in mind that your companion probably fell in love with a happier, more vivacious, and more confident version of you.

Your ex may ponder what happened to the person they fell in love with if they saw you in a depressed, lonely, and desperate state. In any case, they are not experiencing the same feelings as when they were in love with the wretched individual in front of them.

Would you feel like you were spending time with a wonderful person if all you ever heard was their sorrow, argument, pleading, begging, or other attempts to persuade you? Obviously, you wouldn't want to remain; you'd rather hang out with people who are more entertaining.

What should you do if you've already fallen into the trap of imploring or even pleading with your ex to return to you and, as a result, alienated them further from you? Even if you're culpable of frequently calling, texting, emailing, or messaging your ex, it may be possible to mend your strained relationship.

Take The Initiative And Accept Responsibility

Being a leader is essential not only in business and athletics, but also in personal relationships and daily life. People are frequently eager to place blame on others rather than accepting responsibility for their actions. Consider that no one enjoys being condemned or blamed for anything. How often have you witnessed someone in a situation where they are aware of their wrongdoing but have difficulty confessing it due to your condemnation?

Prioritize strengthening your friendship

In the beginning stages of rekindling your relationship with your ex, prioritize strengthening your bond. I believe that friendship is the foundation of a robust relationship, so this is crucial. Consider that when you have a true ally, you do your best to overcome any difficulties you may have encountered in the past. Why? Because this person is your friend, you would do anything to preserve your relationship with him or her. If the friendship is not secure, it is simpler to separate. So frequently do I observe relationships that are motivated solely by sex or money? The foundation of this relationship is as fragile as a structure made of straw. When even the slightest wind blows, the structure will be blown away.

Take your leisure

Don't worry about getting back together with your ex-partner right now. Now is the time to take your time, as there is no need to hurry. Perhaps begin with a text message to inquire about their well-being and how life is treating them. After some time, you can work up to a phone call in order to maintain communication and strengthen your relationship.

Avoid discussing prior failures.

As you begin to repair your relationship, you should avoid discussing past failures. Let sleeping canines lie is one of the worst things that you can do. I've heard it said that whatever you seek will inevitably find you. Regardless of whether it is positive or negative, you will attract that. Maintain a positive attitude and anticipate a better future. If you want to move on and make this relationship work, you should avoid constantly reminding your ex of why you broke up in the first place.

Consider the positive qualities of your ex

All of us are human creatures. None of us is flawless. It is inevitable that we will all continue to make errors throughout our lives. If you examine a person's life resume, you will likely find that they have experienced numerous disappointments, unless they have been living under a rock. It is crucial to acquire the skill of forgiving. I want to emphasize this because I believe it is crucial not only for your relationship but also for you. I believe that holding onto items hurts you more than it hurts anyone else. Have you ever had a conversation with a person who refuses to let go of the past? Have you observed how wretched they appear? They are so miserable because they have surrendered their power to the individual with whom they have a dispute.

Imagine a person holding twenty packages in her hands. You can undoubtedly imagine how uncomfortable this individual would be and how slowly they would have to move while carrying 20 bags. They are exhausted, irritable, and unhappy. I mean, you would be if you were carrying twenty suitcases. This individual has presumably been carrying twenty bags for years. It will likely be difficult for them to lay them all down immediately.

When habits are formed, they are extremely difficult to immediately eradicate. But perhaps we can convince them to set down one bag at a time, and as we do so, you will begin to observe them becoming stronger, more confident, and happier. Over time, they recognize how absurd it was to carry around so much baggage in the first place. I believe your life will be the same if you let go of your burden. Start seeing the good in others. Consider them not for who they are now, but for who they can be tomorrow.

Create a list of everything you are clinging onto (your life's baggage). Perhaps you are unhappy about something someone did to you over a decade ago. Call them up and let them know you absolve them for their actions. You will discover that this is one of the most empowering actions you can take for yourself. After completing this, you would feel as though nothing could stop you.

Invite them on a date.

When you believe the time is appropriate, ask your ex out on a date. This need not be something formal; keep it as lighthearted and straightforward as feasible. You should be familiar with your ex and the activities they enjoy. I'm fairly certain that you both have a favored restaurant where you enjoy dining. There are no conditions attached; the goal is to strengthen the friendship for now. As your friendship develops, I believe your romantic life will also flourish.

www.ingramcontent.com/pod-product-compliance
Lightning Source LLC
Chambersburg PA
CBHW050245120526
44590CB00016B/2227